Jake and Kate Save the Apes!

Written by **Peter Millett**
Illustrated by **QBS Learning**

Fast phonics

Before reading this book, ask the student to practise saying the sounds (phonemes) and reading the new words used in the book. Try to make it as speedy and as fun as possible.

Read the tricky high frequency words

The student can't sound out this word at the moment, but they need to know it because it is commonly used.

their

Tip: Encourage the student to sound out any sounds they know in this word, and you can provide them with the irregular or tricky part.

they

This tricky high frequency word was introduced in Level 3, but you may want to revise it before reading this book because it uses a spelling for the sound /ai/ ('ey') that is not taught in *Snappy Sounds* Year 1.

Say the sounds

ea steak
a-e plane
a paper
ay play
ai train
ea beach
e me
ee bee

Tip: Remember to say the pure sounds. For example, 'ssss' and 'nnnn'. If you need a reminder, watch the *Snappy Sounds* videos.

Snappy words

Point at a word randomly and have the student read the word. The student will need to sound out the word and blend the sounds to read the word. For example: 'g–rrr–ea–t, great'.

ape	cape	mate
safe	came	take
lake	Kate	Jake
snake	brave	shake
shape	save	mistakes
inflate	great	break
day	major	again
delay	hooray	make

Quick vocabulary check

The underlined words may not be familiar to the student. Check their understanding before you start to read the book.

Jake the ape had a cape. His great mate Kate the snake had a cape, too.

They were smart and brave.

One day, some apes went on a fun trip to the lake. But they made some mistakes with their boats.

Boat One hit a big shape. It made the boat shake. It was not safe.

"Help us, Jake and Kate!" they said.

Boat Two hit a sharp point in the lake.
It made a major cut in the boat.

"Help us, Jake and Kate!" they said.

Boat Three came near a big drop. It was not safe.

"Help us, Jake and Kate!" they said.

"We will make this day great again!" said Jake and Kate.

So Jake and Kate came to save Boat One.

"Hang onto Kate," said Jake. "Great!"

The apes from Boat One were safe!

But Kate and Jake did not take a break.

"We aim to make the lake safe," said Jake.

So Jake and Kate came to save Boat Two.

Kate put some air into the boat. She made it inflate! Great!

Then Jake put tape on it.

Jake and Kate made the apes safe! But they did not take a break.

So Jake and Kate came to Boat Three.

Jake swam into the lake with Kate on his back. They made the boat stop.

The boat did not drop. Hooray!

The apes were safe. Great!

Jake and Kate did not delay. They saved all the apes on the lake that day. They were smart and brave.

The ape and the snake were great teammates!

Comprehension questions

Well done!

Let's talk about the story together

Ask the student:
- How many boats did Kate and Jake save? What happened to each of the boats?
- Where does this story take place?
- What is a mistake? Can you use the word 'mistake' in your own sentence?
- Do you think Jake and Kate were great teammates? Why?

Snappy words

Ask the student to read these words as quickly as they can.

Jake	ape	cape
mate	great	Kate
snake	brave	mistakes

Fluency

Can the student read the story again and improve on the last time?

Have fun!